FROM

THERE TO HERE

AND BEYOND

EVIDENCE OF SPIRITUAL WARFARE

Destiny B. Sincere

FROM THERE TO HERE AND BEYOND
EVIDENCE OF SPIRITUAL WARFARE

iUniverse books may be ordered through booksellers or by contacting:

iUniverse
1663 Liberty Drive
Bloomington, IN 47403
www.iuniverse.com
844-349-9409

Because of the dynamic nature of the Internet, any web addresses or links contained in this book may have changed since publication and may no longer be valid. The views expressed in this work are solely those of the author and do not necessarily reflect the views of the publisher, and the publisher hereby disclaims any responsibility for them.

Any people depicted in stock imagery provided by Getty Images are models, and such images are being used for illustrative purposes only.
Certain stock imagery © Getty Images.

All unmarked scripture quotations are taken from the Holy Bible, King James Version (Authorized Version). First published in 1611. Quoted from the KJV Classic Reference Bible.

Scripture quotations marked NLT are taken from the Holy Bible, New Living Translation, copyright © 1996, 2004, 2007. Used by permission of Tyndale House Publishers, Inc. Carol Stream, Illinois 60188. All rights reserved.

ISBN: 978-1-6632-3786-6 (sc)
ISBN: 978-1-6632-3787-3 (e)

Library of Congress Control Number: 2022907151

Print information available on the last page.

iUniverse rev. date: 09/07/2022

Mom and Dad,

Thank you for doing the best that you were able to do as my parents. I learned many things from you, but I made my own choices in life. My choices led me down a troubled life, but I finally surrendered my life to Jesus while you both were still alive and well. I am so happy that I was able to be there for you guys when you needed me. I am grateful to God that you witnessed my ongoing transformation before your transitions.

CONTENTS

ACKNOWLEDGMENTS

In loving memory of my parents, sister, and three grandchildren; with the support of my husband and adult children, I boldly and courageously share my story, from my early childhood and throughout my life, as it relates to my relationship with God. As I expose the environmental surroundings throughout my life, please understand that I do not place any blame on my parents because they did the best that they could according to their life experiences. I am grateful for the many people who supported my endeavors to write a book that exposes my old life and my transformation to my new life through my personal relationship with Jesus Christ.

Every person and event—good, bad, ugly, or indifferent—that was and is a part of my life from the time of my birth until now has helped me to become the person I am today in Jesus Christ, and they have all inadvertently contributed to this book based on their contributions to my life. I am truly grateful for everyone and their contributions to my life experiences. Everyone in every area of my life has contributed to my relationship with Jesus Christ and the woman of God that I have grown to become and continue to become through spiritual maturity as I fulfil God's purpose and plan for my life.

INTRODUCTION

Have you ever concluded that there is no God? Maybe you thought, *If there is a God, He does not love me or care about me.* I was thirteen years old when I came to that conclusion. Ironically, several months before coming to this assumption, I had been water baptized without having a full understanding of what water baptism meant. I believed baptism caused salvation, and that everything that was going wrong in my young life would change after being immersed in water. But my reality was, everything worsened. From the time of my youth to young adulthood, I lived four different lifestyles with my two parents. I lived a lifestyle of a happy family, another of a family with domestic violence, yet another of a single-parent home with alcoholism and abuse, and still one more of a single-parent home with structure and stability. I think it is safe and true to say that I was emotionally distraught and mentally confused. But God!

In this book I will share a little about my life and myself before, during, and after receiving Jesus Christ. Beyond are the goals that I have set for myself toward helping others with their growth and spiritual journeys. It's not important to focus on where we have been or even where we are right now, because it all contributes to where we are going in life.

My setback began when I was thirteen years old and my comeback began twenty-four years later. One early morning, I called on the name above all names. I felt like I was the only person in the world, and I looked up to the sky and said, "Jesus, you have to help me!" I did not have an instantaneous moment of change, probably because I would not move out of the way. But as you will see, it did happen, and I want to share that story with you. My story provides evidence of spiritual warfare and the effect it has on humanity.

This book is organized in sections that I call "episodes," each calling out specific heartaches and milestones on my life's journey. Each episode could be thought of as a miniseries and each chapter could be thought of as a book.

I will show how I began down the wrong path, which slowly made my life worse and worse until I had a spiritual revelation that Jesus was the answer. I made a right turn and discovered that one can apply spirituality and a relationship with Jesus Christ to resolve the problems of life and live according to the peace that the Bible promises.

It is my hope and prayer that anyone who does not know Jesus and the pardon of sin will come to know Him, and will receive Him and the gift of salvation. Amen.

I can say beyond a shadow of a doubt that, through my faith in the Lord, I will not become dependent on anything or anyone other than Jesus Christ. I have developed a personal relationship with God that goes beyond religion. Spiritually, I have found who works for me, with me, and through me, and who loves me—and He is God. I cannot and do not ridicule anyone who does not hold the same belief as I do, but I will share Jesus with anybody and everybody who will listen. I do not pick and choose scripture to live by and adapt the Bible based on how I want to live. I understand and believe that the whole Bible is to be lived by and through the example of Jesus Christ. Therefore, I live to adapt my life to the Bible. (All biblical scripture is for building good character and living a good life under any and all circumstances.)

Without faith, it is impossible to believe, but with faith, all things are possible if we only believe. I had to go through so much turmoil to come to believe. I can guarantee that if you read the Word of God—the Holy Bible—and build a relationship with Jesus Christ, your eyes will be open to the truth as I believe the truth. And based on the Word of God, we make the decision to spend eternity in heaven or hell.

Through my story, I pray that at least one person may learn to trust the Lord, no matter what happens; no matter where they have been, or what they have done, and who doesn't like them, or who does not believe in them. It is my sincere hope that everyone who reads this book, and doesn't know Jesus, receives Jesus and the gift of salvation. Please know that God loves you, so trust in the Lord and believe in yourself.

EPISODE ONE

<hr/>

But evil will come on you which you will
not know how to charm away; and disaster
will fall on you for which you cannot
atone; and destruction about which you do
not know will come on you suddenly.

—Isaiah 47:11

1

SAFE

Happy Home

MY EARLIEST MEMORY OF HOME does not have a white picket fence, a dog, and two and a half children. In the happy family life I remember, we were living on a small street in a row house with a front porch, hedges, a gated backyard, and neighbors with three hound dogs. Our happy home life included regularly attending church, school, and piano lessons as integral parts of my life. I was the oldest of three children, with one brother, Snoopy, and one sister, Misty. Misty was the baby of the "gang." (That was what my dad called us as a term of endearment; we were his gang.) It seems not that long ago … "Come on, gang," "Let's go, gang," "Are you ready, gang?" and "Jump in, gang" (as we were getting in the car).

My dad worked all the time during the week and sometimes he had part-time jobs. After his main job at the shipyard, he would come home and eat dinner. On some nights he also drove a cab, and in the winter, he delivered heating oil to homes. Sometimes my brother went with him to deliver oil. But I remember that he was always home for dinner, our bedtime, and church. He was the kind of father and husband who made sure the bills were paid and we had need for nothing.

Once a month I would sit at the dining room table and watch my dad as he took out his checkbook and the bills from a shoebox and wrote checks. We (my brother, sister, and I) would go to the mailbox with Dad and he would race us home. It was like taking a walk around the block; once we arrived at the mailbox, we would start running to beat Dad home. He always gave us a head start; he wouldn't start running until after he had put the mail in the mailbox. First, he would walk a little bit, as we would see him do when we looked back, but he always won.

On Saturdays, if he did not have to work for overtime, he helped with the chores, such as cutting the hedges or patching the roof when necessary. And Saturdays were haircut days. Sometimes I would go with him and my brother to the barber and watch them get their hair cut. I was a daddy's girl, and so was my sister, but she did not go to the barbershop with us because she was too young. Saturdays were also hair days for me and my sister. Misty got her hair washed while we were at the barbershop, and I got my hair washed when I returned home from the barbershop with my dad and brother. My mom would wash, knot, and later let out our hair to air dry, and then sometimes she would press our hair, but most often she braided it.

Mom was a housewife and mother. I recall her taking really good care of us. She got us ready for school, kept the house clean, washed our clothes, and cooked. But I remember Mom occasionally working part-time too. I do not think it was because Dad needed help with the bills; I think Mom could have been a little bored. I can remember Dad telling us the story about when Mom had once painted the steps in the house pink while she was waiting for him to get home from work. Plus, as we got older, we were responsible for some of the household chores, which gave her less to do.

During the school year, we would come home and do our homework. Anything we could not figure out or Mom could not help with would wait until Dad got home.

We could go out and play until dinnertime (weather permitting), but we did not have permission to leave our street. Many days, my sister and I would jump double Dutch rope in a parking spot under a tree with shade (when available) or play hopscotch in front of the house. We played tag, hide-and-go-seek, Mother may I, giant step, and old Momma witch. Sometimes we would sit on the porch and play jacks. Other times we could not go off the steps, so during those times, we played step games like the devil and the egg, in the clocks, truth or dare, and dumb school. There were also days when both our parents were working, and we could not go outside until one of them was home.

On the days when we could not go outside and play, we would rearrange the furniture and play in the house among ourselves. Baseball, played with a ball of aluminum foil and our fists as bats, was one of our all-time favorite indoor activities when we had to stay in the house. I remember our parents questioning aloud to themselves, "How do we keep running out of foil so fast?" Since baseball was more of a boy's sport, my sister and I convinced Snoopy that he had to play some of our games also. Therefore, he played double Dutch and jacks with us. He was good at jacks but he could not jump double Dutch so we were nice and sometimes played singles so he could get some jumps too. We were good at entertaining ourselves and having fun.

Of course, as much as we loved each other and were almost inseparable, we had our times of teasing, fussing, arguments, and disagreements, but we were always there for each other, no matter what! My sister and I were protective of each other, but we were overly protective of our brother. After all, we could double-team him at times but nobody else had better mess with him.

Indeed, life was pretty good with school, church, Mom, Dad, my brother, and my sister. My dad taught us the Bible, though my mother did not participate in that. He would teach us songs and he had Bible reference books and a dictionary to help him in teaching us and telling us what the Bible was about. I felt so safe … we sat together at dinner, and every night Misty and I kissed Daddy good night. My dad and Snoopy shook hands at bedtime. My dad said, "Men don't kiss." Although we did not say the three simple words, "I love you," love filled our home.

My parents sometimes would get dressed up and go to events such as masquerade balls and cabarets with family and friends. I also remember them going to the world's fair when I was very young. I loved to see my mom get dressed up. I could not wait to grow up and get dressed up for events. I must say that I felt safe and adored throughout my young life. Little did I know that our lives were going to be turned inside out and upside down. No, the enemy did not come in like a flood; he was subtle, discrete, and conniving.

2

SHATTERED

Alcoholism/Domestic Violence

ALTHOUGH I WAS HAPPY AND enjoyed my childhood with my brother and sister, my parents were becoming noticeably distant. When I look back at that time in my life, it brings to mind the image of a stone hitting a window and the window slowly shattering until it is broken beyond repair.

Late one night, we awakened to the sounds of loud voices and thumping coming from downstairs. We ran down to about the middle of the stairway, leaning over the banister and crying profusely, afraid of what we were witnessing. I remember hearing my mom pleading with my dad to stop. When my dad saw us on the steps crying, he came over and tried to console us, but I was now damaged, and I believe my brother and sister were also. Domestic violence is a form of child abuse and causes trauma that could be damaging later in life and during adulthood. To this day I do not know what sparked their actions that night. However, I know that since that night, our family began a downward spiral. I know that Satan is real, and he will use a Christian such as my dad and a non-Christian such as my mom as pawns in his war against God.

I was about nine years old when the happy home I had known began to shatter. I was in fourth grade when I intentionally did something wrong. We would change classes for reading and math. The desk where I sat in the math class belonged to another student and had a pencil case in it. I took it from the desk. I knew that I could not take it home because I knew what I had done was wrong, so I put the pencil case in my desk. After all, I knew that taking something that did not belong to me was stealing, and stealing was wrong. The next day in school, the math teacher came to my reading class and began to talk to my teacher. My heart dropped, and I went to the coatroom, pretending that I had to get something from my coat. Of course, they found the pencil case in my desk and suspended me from going to school for five days. When everyone asked why I had taken the pencil case from the other student's desk, I had no answer. I really did not know why I had taken it, but in looking back, I think I may have hoped that getting in trouble would make my parents act right (according to me, acting right meant the dysfunction of domestic violence would discontinue with my parents). Was that too much for a child to want in their life? Perhaps this was the beginning of my psychological distress. My attention span and grades began to deteriorate. I received my first D on my report card while in fourth grade after getting all A's and B's since first grade.

During the subsequent separation of my parents, I did not do my homework as well as I could have, and I began doing quite a bit of daydreaming in class. I thought that I could do something to fix my parents, but taking the pencil case and getting a D did not help them at all. I now wonder if my siblings and I should have been in children's therapy. Did children's therapy exist back then? Could some resources have been made available to us to help make sure that we were okay through all this? Or was this supposed to be normal? (Although I cannot recall any other families going through something like this.) After all, with all the noise and disruption coming from our house, people had to know, but I guess back then it was just about minding your own business, except when it came to gossip.

But one day, the pressure that had been seething beneath the surface came to a head, and the last episode of domestic violence led to my dad fighting for his life at the hands of my mother. I truly believe that she was trying to stop him, not trying to kill him, but she stabbed him in his right thigh. She did not serve any prison time for the accident, as I can recall, because she had stabbed him in self-defense.

After my dad's hospital stay and recovery, he came to the house and we thought he was finally coming back home. But that was not the case. He entered the house and sat in the chair closest to the front door. When he sat down, he leaned to one side and crossed his legs as if he were trying not to apply any pressure or weight to his wounded leg. He addressed us with his usual term of endearment.

"Well, gang," he said, with an unusual look on his face as he nervously held some items in his hands. "I've tried my best to stay here as a family with you and your mother. But after this incident, I am afraid for my life and I cannot come back home."

The items he held in his hands were gifts for us. I cannot recall what he gave my brother, but he gave me and my sister birthstone rings. He gave us these gifts and told us, "I will continue to be in your life and will visit as often as I can. I can just no longer live here with your mother."

I felt like every part of me had fallen apart on the inside and I was afraid, but I did not tell my dad that I did not want him to leave us. I did not want him to be home and hurting Mom because of who she became when she was drunk. I also did not want her to hurt him because she needed to defend herself. We had no questions for our dad, we were young and really didn't know what to say except, "Okay."

As close as we were, my brother, sister, and I have never talked about that day or shared our feelings with each other about what transpired.

I often wondered what would have happened if I had not run out of the house on the night my mother almost killed my father. I always left the house to call the police for help when my dad physically fought my mother. On that night, I hid on a neighbor's porch and waited for the police to come. My dad called my name but I did not come out of hiding even though I knew he wouldn't hurt me. I watched my dad get into the car to look for me. As my dad drove off, I saw my mother leave the house also, but I stayed in hiding until the police showed up. Apparently, my dad was driving back down the street and saw my mother walking down the street. He got out of the car for whatever reason, and that was when she stabbed him in the leg.

I heard sirens, and I stopped the police and asked, "What happened to my mother?"

The officer looked at me and said, "We don't have a woman in here, we have a man."

That night was the last domestic violence event between my parents. When my mother stabbed my father in the leg, she inadvertently cut a main artery. That night my mother almost killed my father when she was merely trying to stop him from coming after her.

For a very long time, I felt like I was to blame for the actions that transpired that night. When my mother's alcohol abuse provoked my dad's anger, which transformed into rage and ultimately to domestic violence, I ran from the house to call the police to stop the fighting, while my brother and sister tried to stop the fighting. I was always afraid for my mom. I am not sure that the fighting was always induced by alcohol. My first memory of the disturbance is of the banging noises I heard from downstairs, which awoke me and my siblings from our sleep. Had those action led up to that terrible ungodly night? Apparently, the answer to this question is *yes*.

Broken Home

For a little while, everything was okay. I continued to go to school and church. We had breakfast, lunch, and dinner, and Dad came by every Friday after work to see us. Sometimes he picked us up for outings on Saturdays, and sometimes after church on Sundays. When he went to church with us, he would take us to visit a relative before taking us. However, if Dad was not with us, we would catch the bus or walk to church and would then walk home. We had choir practice on Saturdays at the church, and on most Saturdays, we caught the bus to the church and walked home.

A bar that we would sometimes walk by on our way home from choir rehearsal had piqued my attention. The music lured me to peek inside and the go-go dancers fascinated me. I liked to dance, and when I saw the women dancing in the bar, I had a desire to be a go-go dancer. But I knew that I should not want to do that, so I did not share that desire with anyone. However, I loved to dance and sometimes would pretend that I was dancing on stage. It was not because I wanted people to watch me dance. I just liked dancing, and when I danced, it was like there was nobody around but me. Dancing has been my all-time favorite thing to do, for as long as I can remember, from very early in my life.

As my mother drank more and more and my dad no longer lived at home, my life was shattering. In her drunken stupors, my mother was not nurturing or supporting.

Even though I was tall and skinny, I loved to wear miniskirts, midriff tops, hot pants, and Roman sandals.

When my dad came for a visit or happened by my grandmother's while I was visiting her, he would say, "You need to put some clothes on."

I'd say, "But, Dad, I do have clothes on."

And he would just shake his head.

My mother had no problem with my style of dressing, except when she was drunk. I would walk into the house, and there she would be, sitting on the sofa drunk with a bottle of liquor on the floor or in her lap. She would look at me in disgust and call me long, lean, and lanky in her slurred voice. She'd tell me how ugly I was, and that I would never have a boyfriend or be married to anyone to have children.

The only people who heard her say these things to me were my siblings. My baby sister would console me, and my brother loved to use the terms "long," "lean," and "lanky" when we had a disagreement or an argument. He would even mimic my mother's drunken facial expressions. I tried to pretend that her words didn't hurt, but my sister knew better.

I'd ask my mom why she hated me, but she would only look at me and offer no reply. I asked her only once while she was sober, and she said, "Mommy didn't mean it." She did not know what she said or what she did, so how could she know that she didn't mean it?

However, she would do it all again when she was drunk, which was more often than not. What was I supposed to believe? I felt very hurt and was terribly confused. I could remember hearing someone say, "A drunken mind speaks the sober truth." Looking back, I wonder if this was a proper way for a mother to nurture her adolescent daughter. I remember calling on God. "God, are you there? What's wrong with me? Why doesn't my mom love me? If you are there, I hate you. You don't love me. I don't believe that you exist."

Her failure to nurture me and prepare me for adulthood had stripped me of my self-esteem, self-worth, and self-confidence to the point where I began to hate myself, and I did not believe that God existed. And if He did exist, I thought He did not love me. Any dreams and admirations that I once had for my life became invalid. I wondered why, if God truly existed, was my life such a sham and why did my mother continue to allow herself to be in a condition that was hurting me as opposed to nurturing me to become an extraordinary woman?

Furthermore, why would God allow any of these things to happen? The domestic violence, the alcoholism, and the near death of one parent at the hand of another parent. I do not remember hearing things like this in school or in church. Maybe my school and church were not teaching me the truth about life, family, and love. Little did I know that Satan was using my mom as a tool in a plan against me as part of his war against God.

Confused

By the time I was fourteen years old, I was engulfed in confusion. I could not comprehend for the life of me why my mother treated me so badly. I could not understand my purpose for my life. Why was I born? Why should I continue to go to school or church all the time? What is the meaning of life? Is this all there is? What did I do that was so bad that I should endure such hatred? At least that was what life felt like to me.

However, when Mom was sober, she rarely ever remembered what she had done when she was drunk. I never feared for my life and I never thought that she would kill me, although I did ask her once, "Why don't you just kill me?" Whenever I saw her drink or go get something to drink, my biggest fear was that she would hurt me. Sometimes she would tell me that she would not get drunk, but she always did.

Many times, she would beat me with a braided extension cord tied with knots. I did not feel I had done anything to be beaten in such a matter, so I figured I might as well start doing things deserving of the disciplined torture that I received on occasion. I remember one day she was beating me so badly that my brother was crying for her to stop beating me and beat him instead. I cried to him, *"No!* Stay there," because I did not want him to endure what I was going through. He and my sister were on the steps, in the same spot where we had stood while witnessing the first episode of our parents fighting.

Other days she adored me, bragged about me, or wanted me to sing, dance, or play the piano. And there were times when she spoke to someone's mother about bullying me or got in someone's face about bothering me. The inconsistency was deeply confusing. I could no longer continue regular church attendance. All I knew was that something was not right with this mother-daughter relationship. Did she love me or did she hate me?

I praise God for bringing me my siblings because they kept me sane. My siblings and I were each other's strength. Although sometimes we had disagreements and would fuss and fight, we always had each other's backs no matter what. However, with Dad gone, our structured household life had been disturbed. There were times when we had no electricity, no heat, no gas, and quite often, not enough food. I was a little fearful the first time this happened. It did not happen often, and it was not so bad, plus we were not the only house on the block that had to go a few days without electricity. There was not much that I could do about the utilities, but I learned to steal food at the market, and I taught my sister to do the same. Then I learned to steal clothes and taught my sister. So, we had food and we had clothes. I continued to steal clothes until I went to live with my dad. I stopped then because I knew it was wrong and I feared he might let me go to jail. On the other hand, my mom condoned us stealing, but it depended on what we were shoplifting and whether we got caught. According to Mom, there were things that were necessary to steal and other things that were unnecessary. However, Dad always taught us that there is never a good reason to do the wrong thing. We always have a choice!

3

---·••·---

STRIPPED

Helplessness

I TRULY BELIEVE THAT ADOLESCENCE is a most important stage for development and preparation for adulthood. During this phase of life, physical and hormonal changes are beginning, and authentic sexuality should be taught. Nurturing, in my opinion, should involve teaching the child to know their worth and building their self-esteem and self-confidence as they are approaching adulthood. I believe this should be consistently reiterated in a positive fashion to help the adolescent stay focused and avoid inauthentic relationships which hinder maturity and delay a successful adult and spiritual life journey. Therefore, during adolescence, I should have been focused on learning what I wanted out of life and working toward my goal, but without help and guidance, I had no clue what I wanted to do. Subsequently, I searched for worth and fulfillment in inauthentic relationships.

My mom's drinking soon escalated to a new level as she was drinking more often and for more days at a time. In her drunkenness our whole existence would go topsy-turvy. We would try to help her by pouring out the whiskey, adding water to her liquor, or hiding the bottles once she went to sleep. But that only made matters worse for me because I was the oldest and when things went wrong it was all my fault and I had to be punished.

I was so helpless. She was my mother, and I could not physically defend myself against her. The impact of the punishment resulted in whelps and broken skin where the cord connected with my body.

Once my mom would go to sleep, my sister and I would put topical medication on the welts from the cord. Sometimes I would leave and go to my grandmother's or to stay with one of my aunts until my dad got off of work. I could not think of a way to keep her from punishing me. However, when my dad would take me back to her and tell her that she needed to stop, she would be all right and wouldn't drink for a while. Once she decided to drink, she could see the fear on my face, and she would tell me that everything was going to be all right and I did not have to worry. I would be as nice as I could to please her. Sometimes it worked and sometimes it did not work. It always depended on where the level of intoxication took her, not how good or nice my behavior was. She always found something; it could be just because she did not want to see me walk by. My mom found out about a job in a seafood restaurant where I could work on the weekends. This turned out to be great. I loved working there, and the best thing was that my mom was usually asleep by the time I got home from work.

When I was fifteen years old, I went to stay with my dad, but I missed my brother, my sister, and my friends so I visited the neighborhood very often. My dad sent me back to live at my mother's since I had been going back so often. I did not want to be there, but it was what I had been used to. Eventually, all my siblings and I went to live with our father.

Self-Loathing

I began to develop an incomprehensible level of self-hatred. Something had to be wrong with me. I could not understand what was happening to me. I was teased and bullied at school and in the neighborhood about my height and about being skinny. Although I had some good friends, I also had some not-so-good friends. I thought it must be my fault, and I needed to come up with a way to do something about the bullying. I believed if I were not tall and skinny, these bad things would not be happening. I despised my height and I believed that smoking cigarettes would stop me from growing any taller. Since I had heard that smoking stunts your growth, I thought smoking would be my answer to stop growing taller and gain weight. In other words, I believed if I stopped growing upward, I would start growing outward, and the bullying would stop.

I was in my teens when I started smoking cigarettes, but I still continued to grow taller. Because I liked the effects from smoking, I kept smoking cigarettes anyway, even though I continued to grow upward and not outward. Little did I know that smoking was addictive, and I grew dependent on the nicotine. I thought I just liked smoking.

When I looked in the mirror, I did not like the person looking back at me because I thought there must be something wrong with her for people to treat her badly, including her mother. I made up in my mind one night that I should just be dead. I took a bunch of aspirin in what I thought was a suicide attempt. However, the worst thing that happened was that my stomach got very sick as a result. My sister was the only person who knew, and she sat with me while I waited to die from the stomach pains. I do not believe that my sister ever told anyone about that night.

Approximately one year later, I self-mutilated the back of my forearm with many cuts from a razor blade. I can still see the faded scars today.

When my mother saw my badly sliced arm, I told her that I had been jumped by some girls that I didn't know. However, a few weeks later, as she was taunting me about something, I revealed that I had cut my own arm. She shared the information with my dad. He asked me why I had done such a thing, and I told him that I did not know why I did it. Looking back, I think that was a sign that I needed psychological help. I didn't try to hide the scars as I was openly displaying the harm that I had caused myself. I also used to slap myself in the face. Subsequently, I realize today that due to childhood maltreatment, abuse, and neglect, by inflicting physical pain to myself I was lightening the emotional pain that was submerged within me. Because of this, trying to stop the internal pain with external pain did not work at all.

Hopelessness

Before finally moving to my father's home, all the moving back and forth between my parents' homes had left me emotionally distraught, and I didn't think life really mattered. I moved from hopeless situation to hopeless situation and was trapped in a body with a very confused mind. My environment exploited my damaged psyche, and my soul was suffering in a battle I did not yet understand.

I gave up. I could not take it anymore. What was the use? I transferred from academic to business curriculum and from the out-of-area junior high school to the neighborhood junior high school. Plus, I started doing all kinds of mischievous things. I wanted to be loved so I became sexually promiscuous. However, I did not always consent, and I was often sexually assaulted when I did not want to have sex. Yet, I believed it was my fault because if I had not been where I was, the sexual assault could not have happened. During some of my mother's card games with her friends, I would wake up to someone touching me inappropriately. After the third time of this happening, I woke my sister and told her what had happened, and we switched sides on the bed. After that, if someone ever came to our room again, they did not come in when they saw my sister on that side of the bed. My sister was the youngest, and they knew our mom would believe her over me if someone had touched her. If they touched her, my mom's crazy side would most definitely break through. However, because of the way she treated me, I believed that she would have turned it around to make it my fault as though I had attempted to ruin her card game. Maybe she would have come to my rescue, but I did not want to feel rejected if she didn't believe me.

My fraternal grandmother would often tell me that I should go back to church, even if it was not to the family church. However, the behaviors of other people who went to church and proclaimed Christianity were misleading and I wanted no part of church and the people who went to church. I was also teased and ridiculed quite often by my peers when I actively attended church. Often there were one or two people who were nice, but my focus was on the many who were not nice to me. Hopelessness settled deep within me without my comprehension, until many years later.

Although I was the oldest of three children, my siblings and I were very close, and I knew that they loved me. Even in the midst of our arguments and fights, we had each other's backs. However, I found that with other people, even when the positive outweighed the negative, I had the tendency to focus on the negative no matter how small it might be.

EPISODE TWO

We are hard-pressed on every side, yet
not crushed; we are perplexed, but not
in despair; persecuted, but not forsaken;
struck down, but not destroyed.

—2 Corinthians 4:8–9

4

---·•·---

STRUGGLE

Battle of Wills

AFTER LIVING IN MY MOTHER'S alcohol-dependent custody for two years after my parents' separation, my dad gained custody of us. As badly as I wanted to do the right things, I had some bad habits that were comfortable and normal to me, and so for the first couple of years, I continued to cut school. My brother had good reasons to cut school because of gang wars. He was in danger even though he was not affiliated with a gang. So, for my brother's safety, my dad signed him out of school to go into the marines. I wanted my dad to sign me out too, but when I asked, he told me to finish school and said that I could go into the marines after I had graduated. My dad's logic was that I was a girl and had no reason to be signed out of school since I was not in danger from gangs.

Joining the marines was my inspiration for going to school and attending my classes. History was my pet peeve; however, I was surprisingly passing the class. I really wanted to graduate high school and become a marine. I think deep down inside, I just wanted to get away and become somebody with worth because I felt worthless.

I believed what my mother had told me, that I would never have a boyfriend. However, I met a young man, and he was persistent, so I gave in to his charm and I had a good feeling that my mom was wrong because I now had a boyfriend.

My dad did not like him much, possibly with good reason because soon my grades began to suffer. I began cutting school again because my boyfriend accused me of seeing someone else instead of going to school, which was not true. On many school days, I would go across town to his mother's house to spend time with him instead of going to school, or I would cut classes and leave school early to prove to him that I was not seeing anyone else. Due to my lack of authentic sexual nurturing, I had no knowledge of how to behave in a sexually appropriate manner. During one of my visits with my boyfriend, we had sex and I became pregnant with my first child. I was still passing my classes and I only needed three credits to graduate. While I was in my fifth month of pregnancy, in April 1976, I was so happy that graduation was almost here. All I had to do was complete my credit hours and graduate. I called the recruiter's office to set up an appointment to enlist in the marines after graduation.

Unfortunately, the recruiter told me that the marines did not enlist single parents and that I should try one of the other branches of the military. I was devastated, and I dropped out of school because I had ruined my plan. If only my dad would have signed my out when I had asked. Yep! It was really easy to blame my dad for my actions. But I had my baby boy, and he was a joy and the product of what I thought was love. However, the baby's father and I never married and eventually we broke up when our son was two years old. He was my first love, as I had misunderstood love based on my feelings at that time.

I do not think that I was playing hard to get, but within a year, I gave in to another persistent young man. I was on the rebound, but I was not going to go back to my first son's dad even though I still cared for him and wished things would have turned out in my favor. Plus, I knew that I deserved to be treated better although I still did not know my worth because I had not been taught that I had worth. I was a giver and never asked for anything in return, but I expected and knew that I should be treated better.

I believed continued pursuit was a sign of sincerity. Once again, I decided to date, and I remembered that this young man, named Will, tried to date me while I was involved with my son's dad. So, I truly believed that he was sincere because after I had turned him down before, here he was again a few years later, trying to be my boyfriend. So here I was again, but this time I was taking birth control. But I got pregnant anyway, in 1979 I gave birth to my second son. The doctor told me that the only guaranteed birth control is abstinence. I was more than likely told that when I had been prescribed the pills, but I had ignored it or did not believe it to be true. I believe it now, and today I share the same information that the doctor shared with me with my daughters and other young women. My grandmother was not happy with me. She sat me down and had a stern talk with me about having children out of wedlock with multiple men.

Will asked me to marry him, and although I did not want to marry, I believed that I needed to marry him. He had a plan that began with him going into the army. I believed that he loved me enough for us to be together for the rest of our lives. So, I said yes to the marriage proposal.

We were married on May 3, 1980, after he graduated from boot camp. After we were married, he put in for housing with the army. While we were waiting for housing, I continued to live in my father's house. During Memorial Day weekend in 1980, my stomach seemed upset, and I lay on the sofa. It soon felt like my monthly cycle was beginning. As I began to get up, my stomach felt like it was collapsing, and I began hemorrhaging. I called my brother from upstairs to call for an ambulance because I was unable to get up as I lay there bleeding. While we waited for the police to arrive, my brother went to get our next-door neighbor to see if she could help. By the time the police came, I was completely covered in blood but I was able to get up. I changed my clothes but didn't think to take the bloody clothes to the hospital. By the time I saw the doctor and had been examined, he told me that it was just my menstrual cycle beginning. However, he had no explanation for the experience that had occurred.

When I arrived home, my neighbor asked, "What did they say at the hospital?"

I shared with her what the doctor said, and she became upset.

She said, "I believe it was more than that. You possibly had a miscarriage. You should have taken those bloody clothes with you to the hospital."

Unfortunately, it was too late to show the doctor my clothes. However, a week later I began to experience the same stomach discomfort that had occurred previously. This time, I immediately went to the hospital where I had given birth (not to the hospital where the police had taken me). I explained to the doctor everything that had occurred the previous week, and I shared with him my neighbor's assumption of a miscarriage.

After the examination, the doctor said, "I see no sign of a miscarriage or pregnancy." The doctor's diagnosis was bacterial vaginosis and he prescribed Flagyl.

I moved with my new husband to Virginia as the wife of a soldier and the mother of two. I had missed my chance to go into the armed services, but I was the wife of a soldier; I was a homemaker, and I was very happy.

About a month after getting settled in, I found out that the occurrences that had caused me to go to the hospital twice prior to moving were not due to a miscarriage or an infection but because I was pregnant, contrary to what the doctors had told me in Philadelphia. I was upset and a little nervous for my baby because the doctor had prescribed a medication that women should not take during pregnancy. However, the army doctors assured me that the medication would not affect my baby.

During my pregnancy, we had visits from my dad, sister, and mother-in-law, and we went back home often for weekend visits. I didn't see my mom much when we visited home. One day, while I was home in Virginia taking care of my children, I could hear my mother calling my name. I stopped what I was doing, unsure of how what I was hearing could be possible. Was this a pregnancy-induced hallucination? Then I heard my name again. To my surprise, my mother had traveled to Virginia and was in a cab that was driving slowly down my street. She didn't know my address, but she knew the name of the street. She told me that she had been drinking the night before, and while she was under the influence, she decided to get on a train and come visit me. She stayed with us for about two weeks, and it was good because I went in labor, and she was sober and was a great help during that time. In February 1981, I had my third baby boy while my mom was visiting. The best part was that she did not drink while she visited, and she completely potty trained my nineteen-month-old son.

I had hoped that my husband would reenlist and that we would go to Germany, but he did not reenlist. My fear was that if we went back home, our marriage would not survive because he liked hanging out and smoking marijuana with his army buddies—and I told him so. At least while we were away from friends and family, there was no outside interference in our lives. Subsequently, he did not reenlist, and we went back home.

We packed up and moved our belongings to my father's house. We had to go back to clean the apartment after my husband's discharge from the army, so money was not deducted from his pay to clean our living quarters. My sister kept the boys while we went back. One of my girlfriends, Cheryl, offered me a pill to help me stay up and clean. I told her that I was not going to take the pill. The pill was called "Pink Lady," and it was some type of speed or diet pill. She convinced me to just take half of it and she guaranteed that it would prevent me from getting tired. So I took half of the pill; after all, she would not give me anything that would hurt me, and she took the pills herself. That half pill worked wonders, and so did I. Our apartment was sparkling more than it did when we had first moved in. Furthermore, that half pill was my first move into temptation and toward transgressions beyond belief.

As I had feared, our marriage bond began to dwindle. My husband was away from home a lot. I went out with him sometimes to visit his cousins or his dad, but I did not feel very comfortable. I would have a beer or two, but there was nothing for me to do when he and his cousins or dad went out. However, I liked going to his mother's house because she would give me advice for the boys and she played pinochle with me. I do not think she liked me very much, but we played pinochle and we talked. That was much better than sitting around and doing nothing. And my husband usually found somewhere else to go while I was at his mother's house.

Things seemed to be looking up, but my husband saw the weekends as a time for going out. One Saturday morning, I was going out to clean the mess left by our dog in my dad's backyard. My sister was upset that I was going to clean the yard and she told my dad. My dad was furious because he did not think my job was to clean up after the dog. He told me not to clean the yard and to leave it for my husband to do. I believe my dad said something about it to my husband's mother and she did not like the things that my dad said to her about her son.

Shortly thereafter, my mother-in-law found a house for us to rent. My husband told me that he didn't know what my father had said to his mother, but she had told my husband that she had to get him out of "that man's house." When he told me that, my first thought was that she had no concern for our family, her only concern was for her son. I didn't know what my dad had said either, but whatever it was, I believe it should have led her to explain to my husband (her son) what it meant to be a husband and a father. Instead, she found a house for us to rent in the worst neighborhood I could ever imagine.

The neighborhood we moved to was very different from the neighborhoods in which I was accustomed to living. The street was very narrow with few houses and big vacant lots. People sat out in chairs or on the steps. Some played checkers or cards while drinking wine, beer, or whiskey, and a few people would be seen smoking marijuana. Children ran and played in the street and lots. I had no friends or family nearby and I felt alienated from the people in the neighborhood.

As a new member of the neighborhood, I sat on the steps while my children played, or I would visit friends and family with my children when I was not working due to a furlough. Since I did not drive, my only means of transportation was public transit, unless my husband was available to drive me somewhere. Due to the distance of travel, taking a cab was too expensive.

When I returned to work, the day care would pick up and deliver our children to our new address at no extra cost. However, my husband did not want to continue to pay the day care costs and suggested that I ask my mother to come help out. Having my mother come to help us was a good thing for a short period of time. She eventually made friends with the drinkers and card players. She found a couple of houses that had illegal bars, and soon after, she was either not home or was too drunk to watch the boys. She made friends who had grandchildren or children who would babysit for my mom. Sometimes, when I got in from work, my husband was not home and my mom was not there. I would come home to a babysitter.

I had to call out from work so much that I decided to take an early furlough and be a stay-at-home mom. Since we no longer needed my mom to babysit, I told her that she could go back home but she ended up staying in the neighborhood and rooming with someone two doors down from my house.

I have always wanted to do the right thing. I believed that the people in my life needed to do the right thing for everything to be all right. Many things I had vowed to myself that I would never do, I succumbed to doing. I vowed to myself that I would never cheat on my husband if I ever got married; I would never take drugs by snorting anything into my nose or freebasing; I would never allow my children to experience domestic violence or any type of abuse. Because of the things I witnessed and experienced in my childhood, I sincerely believed these things were wrong, and I was guarding my children from these things. However, in my weakness I did these wrong things and brought these negative experiences into my life and into the lives of my children. Jesus told the disciples, "Keep watch and pray, so that you will not give in to temptation. For the spirit is willing but the body is weak" (Matthew 26:41, NLT).

However, I knew nothing about this because I left the church and stopped praying. I opened myself up to be led into temptation that I was not strong enough to resist no matter how hard I tried. The good life I had wanted for myself and for my boys was deteriorating slowly but surely, all because I had no value, no worth, no confidence, and no faith ... I had nothing and I didn't know it. And I missed a God-given warning due to leaving church. "Don't be fooled by those who say such things, for 'bad company' corrupts good character. Think carefully about what is right, and stop sinning. For to your shame, I say that some of you don't know God at all" (1 Cor. 15:33–34, NLT). I stopped thinking carefully about what was right and I made a bad decision because I did not know any better, but I wanted things to be better.

Some people who were already in my life and others that I had allowed into my life would try to make me believe that doing drugs wasn't really bad. They would name others who did drugs, and the most deceiving thing people would say was, "It won't hurt you. See? I do it and I'm okay," or "I wouldn't give you anything to hurt you; just try it."

Although I continued to say no to drugs for years, one day I gave in and said, "Okay, I'll try it."

Escape

Nothing was going right in my life. I was married with children, but it seemed like it was just me and the children. My husband was not home as much as I thought a husband should be. He was not caring for his wife and children the way I thought a husband should. I asked him one night if he had married me just to tell people, "Yea, I have a wife and kids at home." I don't remember what his answer was, but his behavior did not change.

My boys were my pride and joy. I loved them so much. I was always hugging them, and every night they gave me a "night-night" kiss, as we called the good night kisses. I had babysitters, and sometimes I would go out after the boys went to bed. Plus, during the school year, I volunteered at school before going to work in the evenings. This was during the time when my mom was helping. Eventually I was not getting enough rest because I started being out late some nights. Someone caught my eye, and I was now once again doing something that I had never believed I would do. I had an affair with the young man down the street. His name was Trunk.

I remembered the half pill that I had taken to keep me awake, and I inquired about "Pink Lady" and "Black Beauty." I knew that if I took half of one of those pills, it would help me. I learned that they were diet pills, and because I was always trying to gain weight, I would take the pill after dinner at work. After work, at about 1 a.m., I would stop at the "speakeasy" and have a beer or two before I went home. In reality, I was hoping to run into the young man who lived down the street. I would take only half or one pill, and people teased me about that because they said they needed to take two or three to notice an effect. I never took two or three, and one day, I just stopped taking them because I no longer needed the extra energy.

While I was self-furloughed because my mother wasn't reliable to provide care for my children, I found out that I was unable to collect unemployment. One day when I went out to collect the mail, I saw a notice from the landlord. It was an eviction notice; my husband had not been paying the rent. Frightened for my children, I tried making arrangements with the landlord that included putting my husband out, but the plan reached my husband's mother, who opposed her son not living in the house. I had to come up with another plan.

I moved into a house across the street, which was more like a shack. The house was burglarized the night that I moved everything in. After I had brought our belongings into the house, I had gone to my dad's house for the night. The boys were at their grandmothers' houses. When I came back home the next day, only most of our clothes and our pictures were left in the house; everything else was gone, including light switch covers, picture frames, and the *Encyclopedia Britannica* that I had purchased for my children's education. The new man in my life secured the shack the best he could. I guess it was good enough because we had no more break-ins. I really didn't want to live there, but I had no choice. Everything I had tried for subsidized housing had failed.

To make matters worse, I was now in an abusive relationship with Trunk. It was like my childhood all over again, but he was both the drunk and the abuser. When Trunk was not drinking, he was the sweetest man and said he would not do it again. But he did, again and again and again. He tried to stop my boys from doing our good night kisses, but to keep the violence down, I would go up and get my kisses while they were in bed. Only when he was drinking was he abusive, but this was something that was normal for me. Maybe that was why I thought that if I fought back he would stop the physical abuse. In reality, I was living the life that I had learned, but it was different because I didn't fight back against my mother when she abused me because she was my mom.

He was not my parent, and I did fight back. I ended up with my arm in a sling because, while I was pregnant with his child, he threw a two-by-four at me and it hit my arm. This was after I tried to break a wine bottle over his head to protect myself from him, but his head busted instead of the bottle breaking. Sometimes I could fight him off without a scratch, and sometimes I couldn't. The worst that he did was fractured my ribs, and a bone chip from one of the ribs punctured my lung. I was in the hospital for a few days because of the punctured lung. I finally tried to break up with him, but he went on the wagon. He didn't drink for a very long time but then the old men, his drinking buddies, began to tease him about helping me out with my boys and they got to him. Trunk once again began to drink.

The little shack that we were living in was truly falling apart. The water pipes busted in the ground, and I had to get jugs of water from my neighbors for bathing, cleaning, and cooking. The oil tank had a leak and all the oil spilled in the basement, so we used space heaters instead. There was a tree growing out of the side of the kitchen wall in the backyard, and planks were used to keep the kitchen door up and keep intruders out. This was the living conditions for me, my three boys, and our baby girl. Today I know that it was only by the grace and mercy of God (who I tried to convince myself did not exist, or if He did, that He didn't love me) that we survived the living conditions without any sickness or disease. I can look back and see just how much He loved me and my children.

Soon after, my sister and my dad came to help me move out of the shack and into a home. Somehow, at some point in time, I got used to the area and decided to stay. We moved into a nice house a few blocks away on a seemingly very nice street. Yes, Trunk came with us. We had a housewarming party and most of my family attended, including my dad, all my aunts, some of my cousins, and my grandmother. I was employed and happy. I told my grandmother that I was going to put my best foot forward and keep it there. Little did I know that I did not have the power to do so even though I was sincere when I made that statement.

The boys were in school, and Trunk was home with the baby. He helped the boys with their homework and started dinner, and I finished dinner when I got in from work. Except for me going to church, everything was as it should be; it was all good. But there was always a snake lurking.

After my first daughter was born, I would snort cocaine occasionally with Misty. A few people tried to talk me into freebasing, but my answer was always no. I told them that I was not going to smoke drugs. However, I also said that I would never take pills or snort drugs, but freebasing seemed dangerous, and I didn't want to try it. They were persistent and once again named some friends and family who smoked cocaine.

"At least try it," Misty said. "Everybody does it, including Cousin Jewel, her husband, Weasel, and his grandmother too."

I said, "Everybody doesn't do it because I don't."

I didn't try it at that time. I had a nice home, a good job, a bank account with funds in it, my bills were paid, I had savings bonds stored; this was how life should be. I felt comfortable and at ease with my life. Who could ask for more?

But one day, when I came in from work, a family friend was at the house cooking up something on the stove. He took a little glass jar from a large pot of boiling water and began shaking a piece of a wire hanger in the fluid in the jar. When I asked him what he was doing, he pulled the hanger from the fluid and I saw that something had clung to the hanger. He then pulled out a strange-looking pipe and put a piece of the substance in the pipe and smoked it. Here was yet another person who was asking me if I wanted to try it, and to my surprise, I didn't say no this time. I tried it and was not looking forward to doing it again.

After that night, every Friday when I came in from work, our friend would be at the house visiting with Trunk. He'd have twenty dollars and would be waiting for me to get home because he needed twenty more to make a drug purchase. I'd put up twenty, and after the drugs were gone, I would go to bed because I had to get up on Saturday morning and do housework. Plus, I would prepare Sunday dinner, meals, and desserts for next week. However, slowly but surely, I began to do a little bit more, and since I always paid out the most money, I learned to cook the cocaine myself and decided to buy it myself. After all, I didn't need him, he needed me. Rather, he needed my money. Eventually I met more people and my circle became a circle of drug and alcohol abusers.

My family began to disintegrate. My oldest son moved to live with his dad at his fraternal grandmother's house with many of his aunts, uncles, and a couple of his cousins who still stayed at his grandmother's house after my significant other had hit him in the face and caused a cut. I was happy for him to stay away to keep him safe, but I was hurting at the same time because I was incapable of keeping him safe.

A couple of months later, while I was at work, I received a call from my second son that he and his brother had been beaten by my significant other. While I was at work, during the summer, he stayed home with the children, my other two sons, and our baby boy who had been born after our daughter. Our daughter went to the day care at my job. When I got the call at work, I told my son to call the police right away and that I would be on my way home. I called one of my close friends and asked them to go to the house until I or the police got there, whichever came first.

After informing the fraternal grandmother of my other two sons about the incident, she asked if she could keep them for the weekend. She made it seem that she was helping me out since I had the other little ones, but when she was supposed to bring them back home, she called and informed me that she had custody of them. I was not aware at the time that she was not being completely honest and that she had only filed for temporary custody. Now my first three babies and my "night night" kisses were not home anymore.

Eventually, Trunk was sentenced to years in prison for another crime, and I was home with my daughter and baby boy. It was just the three of us now, but my newest baby boy was not old enough to attend day care. I asked a neighbor to babysit for me, but one day I came home to strange people in my house using drugs. The baby was asleep, but I was not pleased, and the behavior was unacceptable. Once again, I needed my mother's help; however, instead of having her come stay with me, I took the baby to her on Sunday evenings to stay with her for the week and I picked him up on Fridays. Everything was good until she went on a drinking binge. I took a leave of absence from my job so that I could figure something out. The company agreed for me to be on six weeks of leave, but it turned out that they needed me to come back to work before the leave was completed. The manager said that I could bring my baby to work until he was old enough to go to the on-site day care.

However, after a few weeks, my mother was back on the wagon, and I was taking the baby back to her for the week. I was still abusing drugs, and it began to interfere with me getting to work on time. I was also trying to get into the union so that I could receive treatment, but I was fired before I was able to get into the union.

I share these details to show that drug abuse and recovery can be implicated and complicated by what and who is around you. One decision can lead to another, and circumstances can create more problems as your decisions continue to be made with the same faulty basis until that is changed. I realize that my abuse of drugs developed into a drug-use disorder, and no matter what negative things were taking place due to the drug use, I continued to use drugs. I was out of control but I was trying to convince myself that I was in control.

As I was watching television one night while the children were asleep and I was downstairs getting high, a commercial came on that asked, "Do you do drugs? Do you need help?" and then supplied a number to call. I stared at that number on the screen, but I didn't hesitate long. I called the number and made arrangement to go into treatment. Guess who I needed to come and help me with the children? I called my mother and she agreed to come stay at the house. While I was in rehab, I got a call from my sister that my mom was not taking good care of the house or the children because she was drinking and was in no condition to care for a toddler and a baby. Once again, I was let down by my mother, not realizing that she had a drug-use disorder as well, only her drug was alcohol.

When I was discharged from rehab, I went home. The house was a mess. It wasn't the nicest house anyway, but things were strewn everywhere. The couch cushions had been slashed and thrown off the couch. Every drawer was open. I had been around the drug scene long enough to know we had been burglarized.

I didn't even want to be there. It was so easy to use drugs and so hard to stay off them. I decided to pick up my oldest son from his grandmother's because they lived close by, and we went to a movie. After the movie, I took him back to his grandmother's and went back to the disgusting house. But when I went home, I just couldn't stay there. I felt unsafe, and I was desperate to escape. I didn't want to be home alone in that awful house. I wanted to go anywhere and was wishing for a hit of anything. So I went to a bar to have a beer. *At least it's not drugs,* I thought. I was in the clear. Except for one thing: alcohol is still a drug.

Eventually I was hanging out with the same people and I just didn't feel it was safe for my babies to be there because I did not know what was wrong with me. *Why do I keep doing drugs?* I was flooded with all kinds of emotions. I wanted to be sure that my youngest two babies would be safe. So I did what I thought was the next best thing, I called Child Protective Services on myself and freely sent them away. I praise God that they were kept together. My daughter was three years old and my baby boy was one year old.

I falsely believed that I would get better and get all my babies back. I told myself a big fat lie. My substance-use disorder had gone out of control. I was escaping something, but I had no idea what need I was trying to fulfill or what pain I was trying to stop. In addition, I was trying to not think about the bad relationships and not having my children, which caused more need to escape. It seemed simple: if I was only thinking about drugs then I didn't have time to think about anything else. After all, I believed all that had been done could not be undone. I was right; what had been done could not be undone, but things could be changed, as I learned later.

There were a few people who told me that I was not supposed to be doing what I was doing, but nobody led me in a direction to attempt to stop doing what I was doing. One person told me that I looked like I should be married to a deacon. That was funny because I wonder if they were referring to the deacon who went to the speakeasy after church or the deacon who deejayed at the bar and sold drugs.

My drug use continued and nothing I tried was working. I even tried reading the Bible and going into shelters, while at the same time I was allowing drug dealers to sell cocaine and other drugs from my house. I was in multiple drug raids, I was held up at gunpoint, I lost my house, became homeless, and lived in multiple places until I burnt my bridges. I lived at my youngest babies' grandmother's house, at my dad's, in recovery shelters, and at my mom's. My memories are very cloudy from 1987 to 1990; however, the clearest thing that happened was my mother's sobriety.

As I mentioned previously, my daughter and youngest son were in foster care since 1987, and in 1990, I received a letter that they were being put up for adoption unless someone came to get them. My mother was legally able to get my children from foster care. She had completed a program, had housing, and was a productive member of society. I knew that God, who I didn't believed existed when I was younger, was real.

However, I continued to struggle with using. I was in and out of the recovery process. I believe that I kept trying because when I first tried to get help, the counselor with whom I was conversing stated, "I can hear a lot of hope when you talk." She told me, "No matter what happens, do not lose your hope." I didn't know what she meant, and I didn't ask. However, I believe that whatever hope she heard stayed with me.

In 1990 I made up my mind to go away for treatment, but I was told I couldn't because I was pregnant again. I had a little help from drug counselors that year, right before I had my child in 1991. But it still wasn't enough. I hated myself, escaped through drugs, and then hated myself again. I felt guilty for every one of my failed relationships as well as for my parents' problems, and for what I was creating for my kids. I began using again to escape, and I tried several treatments in 1992 and 1993. I even took in urine from my toddler to cover my using when I had to be drug tested in 1993. I felt so guilty about it that I dropped out of outpatient treatment. By this time Trunk and I were illegally subleasing my mother's apartment and were living there with our baby girl. My mother was blessed to purchase a house and she and our other two children moved into the new house.

Eventually my oldest son came to live with us at the apartment and my other two boys visited frequently. I was so unnoticeably internally messed up and outwardly I was out of control. We had to move because, once again, I had other drug users in and out of the house often enough that the neighbors complained to the rental office. My baby girl and I went to live at my mother's new house. My son didn't want to stay there so he went to live at my cousin's, and my significant other went to his mother's house. It seemed like no matter where I went, I found people doing the same drug that had me hooked.

In 1994 I again tried recovery and discovered that I had a clinical depression that stemmed from my childhood, which meant I had a dual diagnosis. The therapist explained a dual diagnosis meant that I had a mental condition in addition to the drug addiction. Because of this, both the depression and addiction needed to be treated in order for me to have a successful recovery. Maybe when I had told them about the self-inflicted cuts, overdose of aspirin, self-hatred, and suicidal thoughts, that had indicated that I had a problem other than drug addiction. I learned that because I was not being treated for the mental illness, that made treatment for the drug addiction almost impossible. I was prescribed antidepressants and I believed that I would finally stop doing drugs.

I was doing pretty well. I was making it to meetings, taking medication, I had a twelve-step sponsor, and I was determined to finally not go back to doing drugs. Then the day came when, while visiting with Trunk at his mother's house for the weekend, something happened with him that caused me so much hurt that the only thing I knew to do to stop the pain was to use drugs. His mother tried to talk me out of going. She had an idea about what I was going to do.

She said to me, "Don't let him (speaking about her son) stop you from doing good."

I said to her, "I don't know what else to do. I don't want to feel this."

It was easy; I was in the neighborhood where I had first started using drugs, I knew all the spots, and I just wanted the pain to end.

Afterward I was so angry with myself and I felt so guilty that I did not go to a meeting and I continued to do drugs. I believed that it was my destiny to live the rest of my life doing drugs. I heard a voice say, *No, it is not.* I looked around but didn't see anyone. I believe it was God speaking to me, but the guilt and embarrassment would not allow me to seek immediate help. Plus, I stopped taking the antidepressants, which probably made matters worse because the mental illness was not being treated.

I continued using, and I met a man while waiting for the bus one evening. He offered me a ride, one thing led to another, and we had sex. After he gave me money to purchase drugs for myself, he kept saying, "You don't know what I do," to the point that he was blowing my high and getting on my nerves.

So I asked him, "What do you do? Are you a preacher or something?"

He said, "The title is not called a 'preacher' anymore, it is called a 'minister.'"

I said, "Okay, are you a minister?"

He said, "Yes, I am."

I said, "Well, God already knew you were going to do what you did, and He forgives you, so you need to forgive yourself and stop blowing my high."

He must not have felt too guilty because he continued to call and we continued to see each other. I guess he could have been called my "sugar daddy minister." Sometimes I would go to his church and go to the recording section while he did his radio broadcast. I would also go to the diner with him and some others from the congregation.

Though the relationship with him was flawed, something inside me responded to the hope of God through what I heard at that church. One morning, after being out all night, I was heading to my mother's house. She had relapsed again. I stopped, looked up to the sky, and cried, "Jesus, you have to help me." I couldn't take any more.

About a week or two later, on Saturday, January 21, 1995, my mother was drunk and was really getting on my nerves. She woke me from my sleep and I just wanted to get away and escape. So I called one of my many friends and met him at the bar. I had a few drinks and purchased a forty-ounce beer to go. We stopped and got drugs (he didn't do drugs; they were for me) and went to his place. We talked—among other things—and I put the drugs in my stem and melted it down, but I didn't smoke. I just stared at it. I really didn't want it.

Later I went to my mother's house (hoping she was finally asleep) with my forty-ounce beer, melted drugs, and a few dollars that I had left over, and I put the money in my coat pocket for later use. I decided that I would wait until the next day to go on a good high and then maybe try the recovery process again that next Monday. When I went into the house, my mother was asleep; I was happy about that, and I went to bed.

Flicker of Hope

The next day, January 22, 1995, my mother was very sick from her binge drinking, so I gave her my beer that I had purchased the night before. I knew that she needed the alcohol to stop the sickness. Her need for the beer outweighed my desire for the beer because the withdrawal symptoms for her to stop drinking were life-threatening.

My plan to go out to get high was not what I really wanted to do, so I stayed in the house, played with the children, and watched television. That day ended up being my first day clean. The next day, I told my mother that I wanted to go away but I thought she should go away first. She said to me, "No! You go. I'll be all right."

I left the house and went to a hospital to detox. Although the substance that I used did not have life-threating withdrawal symptoms,

I was able to go through detox because of a heart murmur that I had since birth. While I was waiting for intake, I remembered that I had a few dollars, so I went to the vending machines to get a snack and a soda. As I pulled the money from my coat pocket, the loaded stem fell from my pocket.

I heard in my mind, *Remember, you loaded that up on Saturday night. You can go outside and hit it and come back in.*

I don't know who I was talking to, but I said out loud, "If I go outside and hit this, I will not come back in." I picked the stem up from the floor and threw it in the trash.

During my stay I was diagnosed with clinical depression and was prescribed antidepressants. After the detox stage was completed, I was sent to a recovery house. It didn't matter that I told them which rehab I wanted to go to. I guess they didn't send me to rehab because it hadn't worked in the past, or maybe I was blackballed. I was afraid because I didn't know what to expect. I tried to manipulate them so they would put me out because I knew leaving on my own would indicate that I didn't want to get better. Well, they didn't put me out, and it was the best beginning for my recovery, and I was also in therapy for the depression.

I arrived at the recovery house on Sunday, January 29. The hospital had sent me in a cab with a one-way destination. Once I got out of the cab, the driver left and there I was, standing there without a clue of where I was. It was dark and there was a warehouse, and I was afraid. I went up the steps and to the left were large double wooden doors. I entered through the right door and to my left was an archway opening. Through the archway to my right, I met a gentle-looking man sitting at a desk.

"We were expecting you," he said.

After he verified my name and did my intake, a couple of ladies came into the warehouse and I left with them. I was happy to learn I was not staying at the warehouse; the warehouse was where the men stayed for the program. The ladies' house was nice, but the sick part of me did not want to stay, and once again I was in a conflict that overwhelmed me and threatened my recovery. But I desperately wanted to change. I learned that if I wanted to change, I could not go back to being the person that I had been because that person had led me to this time in my life. I had to become a new person.

5

———•◆•———

SURRENDER

Treatment/Recovery

I HAVE BEEN TO MANY drug detox and rehab facilities in the past that did not sufficiently help. However, I think it was no coincidence that the name of my last detox facility was Mt. Sinai Hospital; the same name of the mountain that Moses climbed to receive the Ten Commandments from God. Although I did not realize it then, I know now that God was present in my life and was moving me to the calling that He had already predestined for me before the foundation of the world (Ephesians 1:4).

For the first week, the policy for the recovery house was not to have any contact with anyone on the outside. I could only go to meetings outside that were for the housemates to attend together. For the first ninety days, the program had a buddy system, and I was only allowed to go for my outpatient counseling alone. The recovery house was coaching me to have structure and stability in my life. I could relate this to basic training in the armed forces, such as in the marines.

I took my duties and responsibilities very seriously. Some of the ladies only had opportunities to be issued weekly chores; however, I was one of the clients who had the opportunity to fulfill every position of the recovery house. After ninety days, we could go to work outside of the program. I was beginning to live life a little bit more as a responsible and productive member of society.

I experienced a few difficulties from some of the ladies who tried to make trouble for me. One day I was fed up with the drama and packed up my clothes to leave.

I told the overseer of the house, "This is not the only place for me to get help and I will find another place."

I was told by the overseer, "If you pack your bags and leave, you better keep them packed because you take you everywhere you go, and you cannot run from myself."

That was the most profound thing that I've ever heard in my life, and it made sense—so much sense that I unpacked and stayed.

That night I learned that other people have no control over my actions. I learned to move the button that they liked to push or not to give them the satisfaction of knowing that they got to me. That was one of the best lessons of my life that I continue to practice to the best of my ability, although sometimes it is difficult.

During my stay at the recovery house, I had visits from my children, but most of the time, I visited my parents and my children. However, I was restricted from going out on Mother's Day because of vindictiveness from the housemother. However, staying in saved me time traveling on public transportation, and all six of my children were brought to visit me at the house for an awesome visit. They also visited me on the day of my graduation from the recovery house. My dad brought all my children to the graduation and I was truly blessed and overwhelmed that they were all with me on that special day.

Attending the twelve-step meetings offered significant support to my recovery process, and even though I had been saved and I prayed first thing in the morning and last thing at night, I still did not want to join a church. However, we only went to church once as a group. I was touched during prayer and began leaping and shouting. My best friend in the house was worried about me and another girl pretended that she did not know me because she was embarrassed by my actions. After that we didn't go to the church anymore as a group. Instead, I would go to church sometimes when I was on a weekend pass when my son or mother-in-law invited me to join them at church. Other than being invited to church, I did not attend many church services.

As I noted, the name of the facility was Mt. Sinai, and Mt. Sinai was where Moses met God and was set apart from the other Israelites. While I was at Mt. Sinai, I was set apart from others enslaved by addiction and substance-use disorder. This story is found in the Holy Bible, Exodus 19. The next place I saw God's hand was in the name of the facility where I went for clinical depression treatment: Friend's Hospital. What a friend I have in Jesus ... I realized that when I called on Jesus that night, a few weeks before going to Mt. Sinai Hospital, I had been calling on my friend. In the New Testament, John 15:15, Jesus calls us His friends.

My name is Destiny, but my nickname was Des. I considered them two different people in one body. My therapist helped me understand that I was not a good person as my whole name and a bad person as my nickname. During one of my sessions, she introduced both names to each other and made them one person psychologically, because I told her that I did not deserve to be called by my whole name.

I blamed myself for so many of the things in my life that had gone haywire, beginning with the night I ran out for help during my parents' domestic incident before their final breakup. If only I had not run out of the house that night! I told my therapist that maybe it was my fault that my mom almost accidently killed my dad because if I had not left the house to call the police, the events would have been different because everyone would have still been in the house. She said, "What if, if only ... nobody knows what might have happened had you not left the house." She explained that it was likely that somebody could have died. She said that I should not be carrying that guilt and I needed to let it go. She would get a little frustrated with me because I would hold myself accountable for things with other people which I had no control over. My oldest son's dad contracted HIV and I told her that if I hadn't broken up with him this would not have happened to him. My first husband was in jail, and I felt responsible because I had left him.

She helped me to learn to love myself and not feel guilty for the actions of others because I have no control over them, just like they have no control over me. Learning about myself, I came to realize that I cannot genuinely love others while having no love for myself. I also found that I cannot love myself without first loving God. I was so desperately trying not to be like my mother that I had no clue who I was supposed to be. *Who am I and what am I like?*

Through the process of treatment, I realized there was so much hurt within me, and I do not think that we are equipped to harbor so much unresolved deep-rooted hurt. Consequently, I was able to face what I thought was everything. One day at a time, I was able to feel the pain, deal with the hurt, release it, and grow from it.

Once I was able to be free from the things that had caused me pain, the time came for me to be free from guilt and shame. I was also full of guilt and shame on top of the pain. I learned that one day at a time is an everyday process that's easier to accomplish with honest and sincere people in my life, people who are living each day to be a better version of themselves instead of trying to be like someone else.

On Thursday evenings, a lady named Sue came to the recovery house for Bible study. By the graciousness of the Christian lady who came to the recovery house and the counseling sessions, the astounding process for my newness was a combination of three treatments: substance-use disorder, personality disorder, and spirituality disorder.

On February 9, 1995, during my second time at Bible study, I decided to receive Jesus Christ as my Lord and Savior and I believed that God (Our Father), is real and that He loves me. Jesus shed His blood just for me, and Our Father raised Jesus from the dead just for me. The best part was that He had been with me all the time, and He still is with me. I know this is true because I survived quite a few dangerous situations that were life-threatening. Not only did I survive my suicide attempts in my youth, but I survived the dangerous situations I found myself in while using drugs. I was robbed at gunpoint twice, I was beaten by drug dealers twice, my life was threatened by a drug dealer, and I had to literally fight for my life one night. My attacker said that I was going to die that night, but by the grace of God, I was not murdered. However, I ended up in the hospital with a human bite to my face, strangulation marks, and knife impressions on my neck. I believe God shielded me from death in each of those situations.

I graduated from the recovery house after nine months. As of the day before going to detox, January 22, 1995, I have not used any type of mood-changing or mind-altering chemicals. After reaching one year clean from substance use, I requested to be weaned from the antidepressants. Praise the Lord, He is a mind regulator. I moved from life struggles and substance-use disorder struggles, as I moved into learning how to live all over again. I was undoubtedly faced with new struggles that I could overcome by the grace and mercy of God. Once upon a time, I did not believe God loved me, and I didn't believe He really existed because I felt so alone. However, this time I was not alone; best of all, I knew God was keeping me, and the twelve-step program was helping me. I believe that because I had cried to the Lord for help and acknowledged His existence, He began to direct me. Until my acknowledgment, I believe without a shadow of a doubt that God was keeping me through everything I've been through.

I have—and will always have—God on my side, no matter what happens in this life. Best of all, I can now see that He was with me even in my doubt, confusion, and uncertainties as I look back over my life. Some people tried to convince me that I was atheist, but I knew there was something, although my confusion led me to be agnostic. I praise God for Sue's love for us and for bringing the Bible study to the recovery house. Her lessons led me to salvation through Jesus Christ and dissolved my agnosticism. Although I did not fully understand, I knew that I was surrendering my life to Jesus Christ because I desired to be better and I knew that Jesus could help me.

Since my graduation, I've continued to work on my relationships. Throughout my life I've had some confusing, toxic, and other types of unhealthy relationships. No matter how hard I tried, there was nothing that I could do to make the relationships better and stay better. I realize today that it takes more than just one person to build a healthy relationship. Although a relationship does not always run smoothly, that does not mean that the relationship is unhealthy. I had to learn—and continue to learn today—how to maintain a healthy relationship even when things are difficult. Mainly I learned that my overall focus must allow me to see the part that I played and what I could have done differently.

Building relationships could go either way; we can build toxic relationships or healthy relationships. I can only be the best person that I can be and change myself even when others do not change. Everyone in my life is not honest and sincere, and it is up to me to distance myself because I do not have to be caught up in another person's drama. I am a work in progress and I am continuously building and strengthening my relationship with Jesus Christ. Things that once bothered me do not bother me or do not bother me as much because of my spiritual growth and because I do not have any toxic relationships. Praise God!

Overall, to be able to establish a healthy relationship, the most important healthy relationship is with yourself. I had to learn to accept my outward appearance. God designed me, and He loves me just the way that He made. I had to learn to not allow the meanness of others keep me from accepting my height. I had to learn to stand up straight and walk tall after many years of slumping and keeping my head down. I had to learn to speak up and be more assertive. However, before learning to accept myself for the person I was created to be, inside and out, I had to accept some profound truths.

My self-confidence and self-esteem were very low because I had based my self-acceptance on whether others accepted me. I had more people who were less accepting of me than the few people who encouraged me even though they were not constant in my life.

Praise God! Many of my companions were fools and I suffered harm, but I've learned to walk with the wise, and in doing so, I become wiser (Proverbs 13:20) and wiser every day. Furthermore, God loves me so much that He made a way of escape through His Son, Jesus Christ (John 3:16). God accepts me for who He created me to be, and He accepts me for who I am as He transforms me. If God is for me, who can be against me? It is through the love of God that I accept and love myself because God is love. His love shines on me and through me and gives me the ability to love others unconditionally.

EPISODE THREE

———◆◆◆———

It is better to take refuge in the
Lord than to trust in man.

—Psalm 118:8

6

SALVATION

Purpose

I DID NOT KNOW THAT after I was saved, I needed to belong to a local assembly of the gathering of a group of other believers, otherwise known as a church. I did not realize that a Christian needed a pastor's care and leadership. I thought that if I prayed daily, repented daily, and continued to let God make me a better person, going to church every Sunday was not necessary, especially going to the same church every week. Therefore, I only went to church when a friend invited me to go, when my son or dad was singing, and for weddings and funerals. I went to a lot of funerals at funeral homes, and I thought that they were just too small for all my family and friends to attend my own funeral comfortably. Some of the funeral homes had standing room only, and at one funeral that I attended, they could not fit everyone inside of the building. I remembered that being a member of a church also provides a church for your funeral. Although I had no specific purpose for my life, two things I knew for sure were that I wanted to live without using drugs and that I needed a place big enough for my funeral. There you have it; church membership was necessary for paying tithes and offerings (payment for your funeral expenses for the service).

Subsequently, I joined to pay tithes and offerings, sit in the pew, and hear the service, but something happened when I joined. Basic Bible boot camp happened. Hallelujah. I learned that there was more to life than joining a church and not using drugs. God has a purpose for everyone prior to their death. God's plan for my human life development began when I was conceived and will continue until my transition from human life.

Those whom God has foreknown, and who have therefore come to Christ when God called, will one day be so transformed as to be like Christ Himself (Philippians 3:21; Romans 8:29; I John 3:2), with the family resemblance as His brothers and sisters. This is my predestiny! I am living a reenactment of the life God ordained and chose for me before the foundation of the world (Ephesians 1:4). God's love is so awesome that He prepared our salvation before He spoke the world into existence (Rev. 13:8).

However, I still did not have any awareness of my purpose for life, but I tried to live differently than what I had learned through the years. Some of me still felt the insecurity of being who I am, and I was still learning to love myself. Learning to depend solely on God was something that I had to work on constantly. I continued some of my inappropriate behaviors such as shoplifting and promiscuity. However, I felt dreadful after indulging. During prayer I realized that just like I needed God's help to stop using, maybe I should ask God for help to stop these behaviors also. When I surrendered these behaviors to God, I was strengthened daily to turn from those ways. As hard as I tried to stay away from relationships with any significant other outside of marriage, and as much as I wanted to follow my vow to myself to never marry again, I met and married my second husband, Kev, in 2001. We met in a twelve-step program and enjoyed going for coffee sometimes before we officially started dating in 1999. We dated for a year and were then engaged for another year before we got married. We celebrated twenty years of marriage in September 2021. Today we continue to flourish in our marriage by acknowledging God first. Kev and I refuse to give up on each other, which has brought us closer together and made our marriage even stronger.

Reset

After being separated from God by my own doing, I had to learn that with God I am set apart from all that I had been led to through temptation. I had to be reset (and stop doing things that provide instant gratification and focus on doing what is pleasing and acceptable to God, according to the principles of the Bible) and learn that my life and relationship with God is unique and unlike anyone else's. For me to find fulfillment is to walk out my journey of fulfilling God's purpose for my life. Sometimes it is difficult, especially when other people forsake me, lie to me, mistreat me, ridicule me, and so on and so forth. I often find myself in a space of dissonance that distracts me from moving forward at the pace that I think I should be moving. However, although I am moving at a slower speed, I always have a revelation that rejuvenates and revives me to press onward.

I share this with you so that you are aware that you are not alone. You've read my story and perhaps you understand some of my choices, or you are making the same choices yourself. Whatever you are going through or have been through, you are not the first and you are not the last. What we must do is make ourselves available to each other and have a relationship with God and others as we were created to do from before the beginning. "… and there is no new thing under the sun" (Ecclesiastes 1:9).

I told one of my girlfriend's many years ago that life seemed like a game between God and Satan. Her words to me were, "It is not a game." The more I read the Bible and study to show myself approved unto God (2 Timothy), the more I understand the spiritual warfare … No, it is not a game. For so long, I was a people pleaser, trying to please man. Man will fail, but God never will. He is loving and just, and He gives us the choice and freedom to have a loving relationship with Him through His Son. Having a relationship with God and living each day to be more Christ-like enables me to have an authentic relationship with all people; although challenging sometimes, it is possible.

I called on the name of Jesus over twenty-five years ago, and my life has been reset. Today I am on the journey of my human life, passing through this land and bringing glory to God and hope to others. I must say that it is not very easy, but it is also not very hard. There is nothing to it but to do it. Of course, Satan will do all he can to distract us with his traps, darts, daggers, schemes, and plots with his imps and his human helpers, but he has no power and he has already been defeated. Submit to God! Resist the devil and he will flee (James 4:7). Command him under your feet (Luke 10:19) and stomp. When I find myself in a trap, I just remember that the blood of Christ has saved me from the wiles of the enemy and has reset my life. It is not always immediately evident to me, but with each day I become wiser and can identify the enemy's tricks sooner and my trials cannot lead me into temptation.

Refuge

I recently learned that some of Satan's weapons are buried inward; not all his weapons are external. Although the internal weapons cannot stop our spiritual growth, they can hinder or slow the process of our God-given purpose for life. I learned that some spiritual weapons that were buried in me were self-doubt and a lack of self-worth, self-sufficiency, and pride. Other examples were guilt, shame, and fear. We should all learn to be aware of Satan's trickery. In war, sometimes mines are hidden weapons that are a surprise when activated. During war, soldiers can see all the external weapons so that they may take cover. As a soldier in the army of the Lord, I find refuge in God. No matter what has happened in my life since I accepted Jesus Christ as my Lord and Savior, I have been shielded and protected from acting in my old ways when trouble comes my way. I continue to grow in the Lord and continue to change.

So much turmoil has affected my life. I tried to take refuge by finding safe places to go when my childhood home was no longer my safe place because of my dad's absence and my mother's drinking. Most often, I went to my grandmother's house until my dad got off from work and he would take me back home. As I look back, I realize today that looking for safety and shelter from the agony of home was only a temporary safety net of refuge. I have come to understand that this time was when the enemy of my soul was planting mines of warfare within my being. Low self-esteem, lack of confidence, low self-worth, self-loathing, and pride were weapons deeply embedded and well hidden.

Through salvation and my relationship with the Father, Son, and Holy Spirit, taking refuge in God keeps me true to my salvation. I am justified by faith, and justification moves me into sanctification. Justification frees me of my sins because they are forgiven. I am no longer a sinner because my sins are forgiven through repentance. Please don't misunderstand, I am not sinless but I sin less. Therefore, I grow daily to have the mind and likeness of Jesus Christ through sanctification, separating me from the way of the world continuously as God continues to do a good work in me.

7

---◆◆◆---

SANCTIFICATION

DURING MY ADOLESCENT YEARS IN the 1970s, I first heard the song on the radio called "I Feel Sanctified." The song moved me, and I jumped up and started dancing. I could not wait to go to the record store to purchase my forty-five-speed record of that song. I played that record over and over like it was the only record that I'd ever had. The song led me to believe that sanctification is based on a feeling, only to find out many years later that people do not feel sanctified, they *live* sanctified. Sanctification follows justification and is an ongoing life process that leads to glorification.

Pleasing God

Once I finally joined a church that I was led to join by the prompting of the Holy Ghost, I met with the pastor and told him that all I wanted to do was to please God. I also went to school for street evangelism, which was led by a pastor who was also a former police officer. During class, the pastor shared with us about when he would pull cars over during his police officer days and he would hand the drivers a tract about salvation. After he had been instructed by his superiors not to give the tracts to drivers, he found a way to get the tracts in the cars without disobeying his superiors while being true to his calling to get the Word of God to others. I also remember that he had a station wagon with a replica of a casket with a corpse on top of the car, and he would drive it through one of the neighborhoods where I had lived. He had hooked up a speaker and would preach the end results of gang wars and drugs. Thirty years later, I saw a television advertisement that he had started a school of evangelism. I signed up and attended the school.

We went to the worst drug-infested area; the drug dealers were informed we would be in the neighborhood and they were not selling drugs in that area on the day of the meeting. We handed out flyers for the meeting location and time. Many people in the area came for the meeting. I was surprised at the turnout. Before the meeting started, people had the opportunity to toss any drugs, paraphernalia, and alcohol they had on their persons. Again, I was surprised at how many people tossed what they had and were saved at the meeting.

However, although I was finally going to the church God had led me to, and I had followed the instructions for new members and followed the prompting to go to the school of evangelism, I believed that I was not pleasing God even though I was sincere in everything I was doing. Something was missing … all I wanted to do was please God. So here was where I met with my pastor.

I was given a test of my spiritual gifts, and my top three gifts were teaching, administration, and evangelism. He shared with me that he did not agree with some of the ways of the evangelism school, and he said that leaders are not natural-born, they must be developed. As I continued to grow in my spiritual walk, I came to believe that my pastor was indicating that while a person can have leadership qualities, those attributes cannot be manifested without intervention to strengthen and extract the leadership skills. I served in a few ministry capacities which helped me prepare for the calling God had predestined before the beginning of creation.

I was a Sunday school teacher, I joined the usher ministry, and I was an active participant in the marriage Sunday school ministry, praise dance ministry, women's ministry, Vacation Bible School (VBS) teachings, food ministry, cell ministry, and more. I truly enjoyed serving, even though I endured mistreatment and ridicule, and I was the only person overlooked twice when everyone had been acknowledged for specific ministries. My daughter once asked why I wasn't recognized, and another time my son asked. My responses to both of my children were, "I did my service unto God, not man." I let them know that I was hurt but that the hurt would not last and I would be all right. What a marked change from who I had been earlier in life when that acknowledgment would have meant everything to me. What acknowledgment? It would have been nice to be acknowledged as one of the VBS teachers and one of the food deliverers. Being the only one who was not acknowledged with the others was a hurtful experience. Once upon a time, because of the hurt, I would have quit serving because I had not been acknowledged with everyone else. However, hurt is not long-lasting. It's only temporary, it will pass, and I will be all right. Yes, I was all right, and the hurt passed.

I continued to go to church and hold my head high. I continued to serve, tithe, and participate, and I found out that faith is what pleases God. It was my faith walk and my trust in God that kept me and strengthened me even when I was hurt. I did not lose heart. I continued to attend through it all until the Lord led me to attend elsewhere for my spiritual growth to new heights and levels in Christ transformed from glory to glory (2 Corinthians 4:1; 2 Corinthians 3:18).

Reaching Others

Sharing the good news of Jesus with others is important to me. I know that I cannot share the truth while living a lie. My walk should supersede my talk. I have heard messages preached that give people permission to act according to old behaviors and sin apparently for good reason if you are saved. However, I have not found this to be true in the Bible. Understandably, it takes time to stop living carnally as a Christian, but eventually, through salvation, the fleshly behaviors must cease for sanctification to be real. If nothing changes, then nothing changes. Continuing to live according to my own ways instead of the way of Christ would cause conflict with others and would make them unreachable.

When I share salvation with others, they will not experience a surprise that indicates I am not living and walking a Christian life. My flesh dies daily and does not have resurrection power. Through faith and a closer walk with Thee, my trust is in God to help me not turn to my old ways based on the behavior and treatments of others, no matter who they are, because Satan uses people as tools in his arsenal to do his bidding. God instructs me to resist the devil and he will flee by humbly submitting myself to God (James 4). Even when I stumble or fall, I repent and get back up. Praise God, falling does not return me to a sinful life. God does not tell us that if we fall we are a saint who is a sinner who has fallen. God says, "The godly may trip seven times, but they will get up again" (Proverbs 24:16).

To successfully reach another, I cannot be a hypocrite. I cannot run lukewarm, and I cannot be a fake, phony, or fraudulent person because my heart aches for lost souls. I was once lost but now I am found, and through it all, I have not seen the righteous forsaken. Reaching others is more than talk, it is allowing the Light of Jesus Christ to shine brightly through me by the way I live and in everywhere I walk.

Purpose Fulfilled

My purpose is not completely fulfilled, and I have quite a bit of work to do while attempting to avoid all evil, which is a challenge because of the world we live and the actions of others, especially when my children are hurt by Christians, from the pulpit to the door. When one of my sons was deeply hurt by a pastor and his wife after years of loving and respecting them, my son was provoked to wrath and I had to remain focused on Jesus and not allow the hurt my son was going through to affect my walk. I had to stay prayed-up. But please believe me, my soul wanted to act out, but I stayed true to God and repented for my thoughts even though I did not act out on them. This is the power of change which God can give you over your life. This was much better for me than being controlled by drugs and low self-esteem. Facing these weaknesses brought me strength, but it was not instantaneous, it is an ongoing process.

I am living a sanctified life that is not based on a feeling. My life is based on continuous change to be more Christ-like, centered, and mindful.

I love God. He is my rock, my fortress, and my ever present help in times of despair. Only through Him can I live a sanctified life of continuous change and service to others. Jesus Christ is my Lord and Savior. He died just for me, and Abba Father raised Jesus from the dead. Jesus is alive and sits at the right hand of the Father. As I continue my journey beyond today, I will live according to the principles of God. I will continue to reap the promises of God and stay seated in heavenly places (Ephesians 2:6). I will never change my confession because I believe the Word of God. To God be the glory. I will serve Him until He gives me the gift of glorification after my transition from life here on earth. The best news is that He loves you too. He wants all these things for you, and all you have to do is accept what He so willingly extends.

He will be there for the hard journey ahead, but you have everything in you to do it.

In my early life I was in spiritual warfare and I didn't know it. I had fallen into patterns that didn't ultimately serve God or me by preventing me from becoming who God designed me to be and then living that each day.

Part of my strength today after therapy is understanding my childhood in a different context. I sincerely believe that my parents' actions that caused me harm were unintentional. I do not in any way condone violence toward another person, and if you are in a relationship that is abusive, I want you to know that it is not your fault, that you do not deserve this, and that you will need help to get out. But I am quite sure that my parents did not plan for their lives to go in the directions that took place, and I believe they loved us the best way they could and sincerely wanted the very best for us. They had their own deep struggles also. The only person who was not surprised by my whole life from birth to now is the Almighty God, the Everlasting Father. Nothing is a surprise to Him; no evil we have done is new to Him or unforgiveable by Him. No matter how bad you think you are or how bad things seem, transformation is available. I often tried to change my behavior and live right on my own strength. Many people look to be reformed, but reformation is a behavior change while transformation is a mind change that will incorporate behavior change.

Maybe you know where you are falling short, or maybe you do not know. I encourage you now to reach out to God and ask Him what you should be doing. Just go to a quiet place. If you don't know what to say, you can say the same thing I had said when I didn't know what to say: "Jesus, I need you to help me." That was what I said over twenty-five years ago, and He's been helping me ever since.

Spiritual warfare is caused by Satan's jealousy of God and hatred of God's creation and love for humans. He looks for anyone with no consciousness of God to keep them from knowing the truth of the Lord. He plants seeds of doubt and confusion by using situations, circumstances, and people as devices of deception. The biggest and worst battle wounds are within, and no one can see them. However, my testimony is merely one of the most powerful life stories of spiritual warfare and God's amazing grace. It is evidence that goodness and mercy follow me, and that His grace is enough. Every battle wound that was inflicted or acquired throughout my life are now victory scars of overcoming by the blood of the Lamb. I want people to know the grace and mercy of our Father in heaven, the love of Jesus Christ, and the power of the Holy Ghost that resides within us is more powerful than every plan, plot, and weapon that Satan can use to defeat us. I believe that God is using me to make a tremendous difference in the lives of others so that they, too, will want to know Jesus and build a relationship with Him.

Overall, I am living my best, most blessed life by the grace and mercy of God. I can share my story and prayerfully help someone. I have a greater understanding of the fact that God uses everything that is meant to harm me and turns them around for my good because He loves me, I love Him, and I am called according to His purpose. The same applies to you. Living with domestic violence, having suicidal thoughts and attempts, being the victim of molestation and rape, being victim to bullying, suffering through mental illness and drug addiction, having low self-esteem and a lack of self-worth, and dropping out of high school are many of the things that were meant to hurt me. And perhaps some of these things have hurt you also. God provides all we need to have a future and a hope.

CONCLUSION

In conclusion, all that has happened in my life is behind me and cannot be changed. So where am I today? I am married to my soul mate, and as I conclude this book, we are celebrating twenty years of marriage. Our marriage is like a beautiful bed of roses; beautiful to the eyes and nose, but every now and then a thorn causes a little pain that we get through with the help of the Lord. Our marriage consists of *no* domestic violence, and we learn every day that we don't have to be in agreement all the time. We continue to grow in our love for each other and we continuously overcome every obstacle, situation, and circumstance that causes any negative reactions and outcomes from our learned behaviors.

Furthermore, I have earned my GED, two undergraduate degrees, and three graduate degrees. I am an ordained minister and the founder of a Christian nonprofit organization. Through the grace of God I am an example to my family, friends, and children who have seen me at my worst, and to my grandchildren who have only seen me at my best, and I am getting better and better. I have come a long way and I have a long way to go! I might not be where I want to be, and I might not be where others think I should be, but Praise God, Hallelujah, I am not where I used to be. I am even better today than I was yesterday. Continued growth keeps me from going astray and helps me to continue moving forward.

Sometimes my flesh tries to rise, and I simply tell my flesh that it does not have resurrection power. The old me is dead and dies daily, as repentance is a daily reprieve—morning and night, and on some days, up to a couple of times during the day—because repentance is included in every prayer so that I can go boldly to the throne of grace, holy and righteous without a spot or blemish, to make my request known to God.

God gave me the strength and courage to overcome and have victory over these things and be the cure for someone else who has experienced or is experiencing life's difficulties. This is my beyond, and God has a beyond for you too. God did it for me and He can do it for you. Satan's traps cannot hold you; you can overcome, rise, and be victorious just like I did.

Speak life! I've included scriptural affirmations to help throughout the day, and information for self-help. Whatever condition or situation you might be facing, whether you are a victim or a perpetrator, we all need the Lord's help. Please check the appendix for helpful resources, and refer to the affirmations and biblical scripture references in the pages following the prayer. I pray that you find these helpful as you begin your new life process.

Note: Please excuse any unintended missed or overlooked errors during the process of completing this book/memoir.

Special note: If you are not saved and would like to receive the gift of salvation, pray the simple prayer below, find a good Bible-teaching local assembly church (ask the Lord to guide you), attend regular services, and join a service ministry in your God-led local assembly.

Prayer

Heavenly Father,

I come to You now, in the name of Jesus. I want to know You better and Your purpose for my life. I repent from my wicked ways, and I am sorry for sinning against You. I believe You love me and gave Your Son, Jesus, as a sacrifice for my life. Thank You, Jesus, for being my friend and for loving me so much. I believe that You died and rose on the third day just for me. Jesus, I invite You to come into my heart and help me begin to be a better person. I want to establish a relationship with You and grow in You. Lord, guide me to a church with leaders who will help me on my journey to be less like me and more like Christ with honest Bible teachings of the absolute truth of God's Word. In Jesus's name, Amen.

AFFIRMATIONS AND BIBLICAL SCRIPTURE REFERENCES

Positive thoughts and affirmations can help you live a happier and more fulfilled life. Here are a few daily affirmations for your personal empowerment, to reach your full potential, improve your self-esteem, and help you break cycles that are blocking your happiness. After all, the joy of the Lord is your strength (Nehemiah 8:10). Make sure to read at least one Bible affirmation and scripture reference daily and say them aloud. The tongue has the power of life and death (Proverbs 18:21).

- I try to spend time with wise people. This helps me become even wiser. (Proverbs 13:20)
- God blesses me with peace and gives me strength. (Psalm 29:11)
- As I cast my cares and burdens to God, He sustains me and I have peace. (Psalm 55:22)
- I am not afraid or discouraged because God goes before me and is always with me. (Deuteronomy 31:8)
- My negative feelings don't come from God so I don't have to put up with them! (2 Timothy 1:7)
- When Jesus knocks on my heart's door I hear him, let him in, and have fellowship with him. (Revelation 3:20)
- I have a living hope through the resurrection of Jesus from the dead. (1 Peter 1:3)

Bible Affirmations

- When I cry to God for relief from the deepest pits of my life, he hears me. (Lamentations 3:55–56)
- When I'm distressed, I cry to God for help and he hears my voice. (Psalm 18:6)
- Though I have not seen the resurrected Christ, I believe in Him and am therefore blessed. (John 20:29)
- I am protected by the name of Jesus. (John 17:12)

Strength Bible Affirmations

- God's power works best in my weakness. (2 Corinthians 12:9)
- Because I place my hope in the Lord my strength is renewed. (Isaiah 40:31)
- I am able to keep my ways pure, but only by living according to God's Word. (Psalm 119:9)
- God is faithful. He'll complete the good work that he has begun in me. (Philippians 1:6)
- I give my anxieties to God and know that he'll take them because he loves me. This gives me peace. (1 Peter 5:7)
- I have life, now and eternally, because of God's grace. It's not because of anything I have done. (Ephesians 2:8–9)

Hope Bible Affirmations

- My God meets all my needs. (Philippians 4:19)
- God is my refuge and strength … always ready to help me in times of trouble. (Psalm 46:1)
- God gives me strength when I am weary and increases my power when I am weak. (Isaiah 40:29)

- God is able to do immeasurably more in my life than I could ever imagine. (Ephesians 3:20)
- I experience true life when I deny myself, turn from my selfish ways, and follow Jesus. (Matthew 16:24–25)
- I have the anointing of Jesus, through the Holy Spirit. He teaches me truth and empowers me to live a full life. (1 John 2:27)
- I love God's principles and meditate on them all day long. (Psalm 119:97)
- I live by faith, not by sight. (2 Corinthians 12:7)
- The same love that God has for Jesus is in me. (John 17:26)
- I can approach God directly with freedom and confidence through faith in Jesus. (Ephesians 3:12)
- As I give up control, release my life to God, and allow Jesus to live through me, God-sized things happen. (Galatians 2:20)

Provider Bible Affirmations

- As I follow Jesus and walk in his Way of Holiness, gladness and joy overtake me. (Isaiah 35:8–10)
- The Lord is my good Shepherd. He provides for all my needs. (Psalm 23:1)
- I continue to work out my full salvation as God works in me according to his good purpose. (Philippians 2:12–13)
- When I humble myself before God in prayer, he hears me and I gain understanding. (Daniel 10:12)

Abundance Bible Affirmations

- Experiencing God and his truths, not knowledge about him and them, gives me abundant *life*. (John 17:3)
- I give thanks to God because he is good and his love endures forever. (Jeremiah 33:11)
- God forgives my wrongdoings and never remembers my sins. (Hebrews 8:12)
- I don't act thoughtlessly, but try to understand what the Lord wants me to do. (Ephesians 5:17)
- God's Spirit in me is greater than any other spirit in the world. He enables me to live a victorious life. (1 John 4:4)
- The Holy Spirit helps me understand God's truth when I read the Bible. (John 16:12)

Make sure to read an affirmation and reference a Bible verse daily!

It is my sincere prayer that this book leads you to a life
of hope and purpose in Jesus Christ. Amen.

APPENDIX

Sometimes life can be so overwhelming, and we want to be better and get better. However, no matter what we try on our own, it is not helping. We do not have to do life alone. God is our ultimate Source. He provides resources to help us get to Him. Below is a list of national resources and phone numbers for help and self-help facilities and groups. They can connect you with the necessary resources in your area for safe, free help online or on the phone so that you can let the healing process begin and find your way to a relationship with God.

For emergency assistance, please call 911.

National Helpline Database
(Provides 24/7 access numbers for various needs.)

Substance Abuse and Mental Health Services Administration (SAMHSA) National Helpline
(Provides information and referrals if you or a loved one are facing mental health and/or substance use issues.)
1-800-662-HELP (4357)
https://www.verywellmind.com/national-helpline-database-4799696

National Domestic Violence Hotline
1-800-799-7233
https://www.thehotline.org

National Sexual Assault Hotline
(Confidential, available 24/7.)
1-800-656-HOPE (4673)
https://www.rainn.org

National Child Abuse Hotline
1-800-4-A-CHILD (422-4453)
https://www.childhelp.org

National Drug Abuse & Addiction Hotline
1-844-289-0879
https://drughelpline.org

Made in the USA
Middletown, DE
16 October 2023

40944168R00057